AT THE
CONTROLS

Women in Aviation

AT THE CONTROLS

Women in Aviation

Carole S. Briggs

LERNER PUBLICATIONS COMPANY
MINNEAPOLIS

*Front cover: Captains Susan D. Rogers,
Connie J. Engel, and Mary E. Donahue at
Williams Air Force Base, Arizona, in 1977.
They were among the first ten women ever
to graduate from Air Force undergraduate
pilot training.*

To my favorite pilot, my husband, Carter

Library of Congress Cataloging-In-Publication Data

Briggs, Carole S.
    At the controls : women in aviation / Carole S. Briggs.
       p.   cm.
    Includes index.
    Summary: Profiles four female aviators: Jackie Cochran, Sheila
Scott, Jerrie Cobb, and Bonnie Tiburzi. Also describes the Ninety-
Nines association of female pilots, and the record-setting flights
of Amelia Earhart, Beryl Markham, and other female aviation
pioneers.
    ISBN 0-8225-1593-8 (lib. bdg.)
    1. Women air pilots—Juvenile literature [1. Women air pilots.
2. Air pilots.] I. Title.
TL547.B74   1990
629.1'092'2—dc20
[B]
[920]   90-6495
                                                CIP
                                                 AC

Manufactured in the United States of America

2   3   4   5   6   7   97   96   95   94   93   92

ACKNOWLEDGMENTS
    The author wishes to thank the following individuals and
organizations: Mary O'Neill, American Airlines; Eddie R.
Hadden, Organization of Black Airline Pilots; Virginia
Oualline, Ninety-Nines, Inc.; Mike Gentry, NASA; Carter M.
Ayres for technical assistance; Dennis Parks, Boeing
Aeronautical Library, Experimental Aircraft Association.
Special thanks to my editor, Margaret Goldstein, for invaluable
editorial suggestions.

CONTENTS

Flying her distinctive Beechcraft Bonanza, Ninety-Nine Pat McEwen of Wichita, Kansas, won the All-Women Transcontinental Air Race in 1969.

THE NINETY-NINES
An International Association of Female Pilots

About 100 women were licensed to fly in the United States in 1929, and there was a lot of camaraderie among these competitive and daring pilots. The first Women's Air Derby was held that year, bringing women together from all over the United States. The race took nine days; the pilots flew from Santa Monica, California, to Cleveland, Ohio. Participants flew from sunup to sundown and refueled at designated stops along the way. Louise Thaden won the race, Gladys O'Donnel came in second, and Amelia Earhart was third.

After the race, several women, including Louise Thaden and Amelia Earhart, decided to start a formal organization to bring female aviators together for friendship and support.

Membership was open to any licensed female pilot. Ninety-nine women responded to the first call for members, so they named their group the Ninety-Nines. Today the group has 6,500 members worldwide.

The first meeting of the Ninety-Nines took place in a hangar at Curtiss Airport in Valley Stream, New York, on November 2, 1929. The 26 women who attended took their refreshments from a four-wheeled cart normally used to hold tools. They shouted to each other above the din of an aircraft engine that was being tested in the hangar. Louise Thaden acted as secretary and conducted the meetings until 1931, when Amelia Earhart was elected as the group's first president. Like all the other Ninety-Nines, Earhart

The Ninety-Nines gather for their first meeting, which was held in an airplane hangar. Amelia Earhart (with striped collar) is in the back row, seventh from the left.

encouraged young girls to dream big, especially if aviation was part of that dream. She felt that the sooner large numbers of women became pilots, the sooner women could become an important force in aviation.

In March 1947, the Florida chapter of the Ninety-Nines sponsored the first All-Women Air Show. Thirteen thousand people watched as Marge Hurlburt set a new international women's record of 337 miles per hour (539 kilometers per hour) over a three-mile (4.8 km) course in her clipped-wing Corsair. Other events were sailplane flying, aerobatic competition, and the first All-Women Transcontinental Air Race (AWTAR).

The AWTAR originated when the Los Angeles chapter of the Ninety-Nines flew to the 1947 Air Show. For fun, the Los Angeles women decided to make their trip a race. The winner, a pilot named Carolyn West, made the flight from Palm Springs, California, to Tampa, Florida, in 21 hours and 45 minutes — averaging 102 miles per hour (163 km/h). After that, the race became an annual event organized by the Ninety-Nines. The women flew different routes across the continent every year.

The AWTAR was the oldest, longest, and largest air race for women in the world. Unfortunately, the AWTAR was discontinued in 1976. At that time there was a gasoline shortage in the United States, and fuel was expensive. In addition, the race was getting so large that it was almost impossible to accommodate the hundreds of entrants at each stop. Finally, the constant search for funding to support the race had gotten to be too large a burden for the Ninety-Nines. Names of each year's AWTAR winners are found on the trophies in the National Air and Space Museum at the Smithsonian Institution in Washington, D.C.

Another project sponsored by the Ninety-Nines, called the Air Marking Program, began in 1935. The program was started because early pilots didn't always have radios in their aircraft, and their charts were not always reliable. To keep pilots from getting lost, the Ninety-Nines painted location signs in large white letters on tops of warehouses, drag strips, water towers, and airport terminals.

In 1939 the Ninety-Nines established a scholarship as a memorial to their first president. The Amelia Earhart Scholarship was created to strengthen women's place in aviation by giving financial help for advanced flight training to selected women. Later, the Ninety-Nines established the Amelia Earhart Research Scholar Grant, which awards research money to an aviation scholar.

The Ninety-Nines have also become involved in projects to help those in need. In 1976 Ninety-Nine Janie Postelthwaite and her husband Hartley cofounded the Happy Flyers, an international organization of amateur radio operators (hams) and pilots. One of the group's main purposes is to help lead rescuers to airplane crash sites quickly, especially in remote places like the mountains.

The Ninety-Nines also sponsor "blood

These Ninety-Nines are painting a location sign, which will help guide pilots in flight.

flights" for the American Red Cross. After people donate blood, it must be processed within four hours. This is often impossible if the blood comes from a community far from a processing center. In 1975 the Minnesota Ninety-Nines began flying blood from small towns to larger cities for processing. This arrangement benefited the Red Cross and also allowed the women to build up flying time and qualify for advanced aviation ratings.

Public education is another priority of the group. The Ninety-Nines maintain a resource center and a library at the Will Rogers Airport near Oklahoma City. In addition, they sponsor seminars on aviation safety and work with schools and youth groups to develop programs and courses designed to give students a better understanding of aviation.

Pauline Gower and the other female Air Transport Auxiliary pilots sometimes faced enemy fire as they flew airplanes from factories to military depots in Great Britain.

BARNSTORMERS
AND FERRY PILOTS

In the early 1900s, flying was extremely dangerous. Crashes were common because pilots didn't know very much about aeronautics. Pilots flew in open cockpits, without seat belts to hold them in. Sometimes they even fell out when their flimsy aircraft unexpectedly turned over in a spin.

Because many male pilots feared that the so-called "weaker sex" would panic in these emergencies, they declared women unfit to be pilots. But most female pilots, like their male counterparts, saw the danger in flying as a challenge and refused to be discouraged. To earn a living in aviation, many women set up their own air shows and did stunt flying, or "barnstorming," before large crowds of people. The crowds not only loved to witness daring and difficult stunts, they also enjoyed the novelty of watching a female barnstormer.

For other female pilots, the thrill came from breaking aviation distance and speed records. Airplane manufacturers often gave free gas and use of an airplane to pilots who were trying to break records. The airplane makers were generous because if a pilot set a new aviation record, it would bring enormous publicity to the company that made the airplane.

Women Take to the Air

In 1910 a New York journalist named Harriet Quimby became the first licensed female pilot in the United States. Quimby was also determined to be the first woman

11

to pilot an airplane across the English Channel. On April 16, 1912, the flamboyant Quimby, wearing a purple silk flying suit, climbed aboard her white Blériot monoplane —a flimsy aircraft that looked like a kite with wings—and took off from Dover, England. Soon she was 1,500 feet (450 meters) into the air and flying through dense fog. Going off course, even by as little as five miles (8 k), would take Quimby out over the North Sea with no place to land. But Quimby used her compass well and stayed on course. Twenty minutes later, she flew out of the fog and landed on a beach outside of Hardelot, a fishing village in northern France. Sadly, she had less than three months to

enjoy her triumph. On July 1, 1912, Quimby went flying with the manager of an upcoming aviation meet. Both were thrown from Quimby's airplane when it spun into Dorchester Bay, near Boston. They died instantly. Ironically, Quimby's airplane righted itself and landed with little damage.

Another early female aviator was Katherine Stinson. Stinson was a barnstormer, an airmail carrier, and an aviation record setter. Born in 1893, the oldest of four children, the tiny woman with the big smile began performing aviation stunts to pay for music lessons. Stinson announced that she could do any stunt that a man could do, but her most famous stunt, the "dippy twist loop,"

Harriet Quimby prepares to take off across the English Channel.

was her own invention. In this stunt, she made the airplane *loop*, or turn in a complete vertical circle, and flip wing-over-wing at the same time. As part of her air show, she also did skywriting by attaching magnesium flares to her airplane.

One day in 1913, when Stinson was performing at a fair near Helena, Montana, the postmaster asked her to fly an airmail route from the fairgrounds to the center of the city. Stinson thus became the first female pilot to carry mail by air.

This fearless pilot also performed stunts in China and Japan using a *biplane* — an aircraft that has one set of wings over its body and another set underneath. Women in China and Japan had never seen a female pilot, and Stinson inspired several Asian women to become flyers. When the United States entered World War I, Stinson volunteered to become a fighter pilot. But the military would not accept women. So instead, Stinson flew for Red Cross and Liberty Loan fund drives. She flew from Buffalo, New York, to Washington, D.C., dropping cards that asked people to make contributions to the war effort. Later on, she worked as an ambulance driver for the Red Cross in England and France.

Stinson also helped her mother and her sister Marjorie run a flight school in San Antonio, Texas. In 1917 and 1918 she set several distance records. In 1920 Stinson retired from flying when influenza permanently damaged her health. She was just 25.

Katherine Stinson thrilled audiences in Asia with her daring aviation stunts.

Bessie Coleman had to go to France to get her pilot's license because American flight schools wouldn't accept black students until the 1930s.

A Pioneer Among Black Flyers

For Bessie Coleman, born in 1896 in Atlanta, Texas, obtaining a pilot's license was extremely difficult. Her family was against the idea, and flight schools in the United States would not accept black students.

Bessie picked cotton in Texas to earn money for college. After one semester, she ran out of money and moved with her family north to Chicago. She soon tired of her work in a beauty parlor and her next job in a restaurant. She studied French and then set off for France for flying lessons. There she earned her pilot's license in 1922 and came back to the United States to earn a living as a stunt pilot.

As the only black female pilot in the United States, Bessie Coleman drew large crowds at a series of flying exhibitions. Coleman hoped to start a school for black pilots one day, but in 1926, she was killed in an airplane crash as she practiced stunts for an upcoming air show.

It was not until 1939 that black students were allowed to enter civilian flight schools in the United States. One of the first black women to be licensed in the United States was Willa B. Brown. She lived in the Chicago area and operated the Coffey School of Aeronautics. Located at Harlem Airport in west Chicago, the flight school trained black civilian and fighter pilots. Although black male fighter pilots were sent into combat in April 1943, the first black women did not graduate from the U.S. Air Force Academy until 1980.

Amelia Earhart encouraged women to pursue their dreams of flying.

The Record Setters

As the 1920s came to an end, pilots became more interested in setting aviation records, and barnstorming became less popular. In 1929 the Fédération Aéronautique Internationale (FAI), an organization that verifies world records in aviation, established a separate category for record-setting flights made by women. Until then, the FAI had listed women's records only as "miscellaneous air performances."

In 1931 Ruth Nichols flew to 28,743 feet (8,623 m) to set an altitude record in a Lockheed Vega. And sitting on top of what amounted to a huge fuel tank with wings, French aviator Maryse Bastié set an endurance record on September 3, 1930, by staying in the air for 37 hours and 55 minutes.

Perhaps the most sought-after women's distance record of that time was the first Atlantic Ocean crossing. Amelia Earhart had crossed the Atlantic as a passenger in 1927, becoming the first female to do so. Although she received a lot of recognition for her courage, this highly skilled aviator wanted to cross the Atlantic as a pilot.

On May 20, 1932, at 7:12 P.M., Earhart took off from Newfoundland in a red Lockheed Vega. The trip was full of calamities. First Earhart's *altimeter*, the instrument that measures altitude over land and sea, broke. Then Earhart flew into a storm and was almost struck by lightning. No sooner had she taken the airplane above the storm than the air turned very cold, and the Vega's wings began to ice up. To melt the ice, Earhart was forced to fly lower into warmer air—and back into the storm. All night long, strong winds shook the airplane. By now the gas gauge was not working either, and Earhart had no idea how much fuel was left. Finally, after a seemingly endless 15 hours and 18 minutes, Earhart landed in Ireland. She went down in history as the first woman to fly an airplane across the Atlantic Ocean. She also became the first person of either sex to fly solo over the Pacific Ocean from Hawaii to California.

In 1937 Amelia Earhart attempted to become the first pilot—male or female—to fly around the world at the equator. Thirty days and 22,000 miles (35,200 km) into the trip, she and her navigator, Fred Noonan, disappeared somewhere between New Guinea and Howland Island. Earhart had been radioing for several hours; she and Noonan could not find Howland Island in the fog, and their fuel supply was running low. The U.S. Navy organized the largest search in its history and kept it up for 16 days. Not a single trace of the flight was found at that time. As late as 1992, people were still finding plane wreckage that might be from Earhart's aircraft.

Saddened by the loss of Earhart, but not stopped, female pilots kept up their relentless attack on distance records. Amy Johnson was Britain's answer to Amelia Earhart. In 1930, Johnson flew solo, or alone, from England to Australia in 19½ days, setting another women's distance record.

Another important record was broken by a 33-year-old Englishwoman living in Kenya. Her name was Beryl Markham. Originally a horse trainer, Markham discovered that she liked flying when she went on a flight with a pilot friend in 1930. After eight hours of flying lessons, Markham had earned her private pilot's license. A year and a half later, she began to earn a living as a bush pilot—carrying mail, passengers, and medical supplies from Nairobi, Kenya, to safaris and mining settlements throughout East Africa. To gain experience in distance flying and

navigating, Markham also made four trips from Africa to London.

In 1936 Beryl Markham felt ready to make the most challenging flight of her life—across the Atlantic Ocean from east to west. Since she would be heading into the wind, the crossing would be difficult. Markham arrived at Abingdon Airport in England on September 1 amidst 30 mile-per-hour (48 km/h) westerly winds and dense fog. After four days of waiting for clear weather, she would stay on the ground no longer. "Neck or nothing," she was quoted as saying. This was Markham's way of saying that she was willing to risk even her life for the record. Much to the dismay of those who loved her, the stubborn Markham refused to take a life jacket. She took off from Abingdon on September 4, 1936, at about 9:00 P.M.

For 19 lonely and exhausting hours, Markham flew blindly through fog and rain. She had only the aircraft's instruments to guide her through the darkness. Since she left after dark and flew "west with the night," she never caught up with the daylight.

Her original goal was to land at Floyd Bennett Field in Long Island, New York. But as she approached Nova Scotia in the darkness, her engine failed. She began a dead-stick glide—a landing without power. She touched ground and felt her wheels sink into the muddy coast. The airplane fell forward, its nose sinking into the mud. Markham hit the windshield hard. Dazed and bleeding, she emerged from the airplane and looked at her watch. She had made the crossing in 21 hours and 25 minutes.

It was not the dignified or celebrated landing she had hoped for, but Markham had become the first woman to fly the North Atlantic solo from east to west and the first person to fly solo from England to North America nonstop. If commercial aviation was to succeed, then pilots not only had to fly from North America to Europe, they had to fly back again—in spite of strong headwinds. Markham's flight helped prove that this was possible. With the advent of World War II, Markham returned to horse training in Africa. Pilots and gasoline were needed for the war effort, not for setting records. Beryl Markham died of pneumonia in Kenya, on August 3, 1986. She was nearly 84.

For early aviators, injuries, and even death, sometimes came with the job. Beryl Markham (above) displays a bandaged gash—the result of her emergency landing in Nova Scotia. Amy Johnson (left) was killed while working as a transport pilot during World War II.

Female Pilots Assist the War Effort

Up until World War II, female flyers were known primarily as record setters. But when everyone turned their attention to the war effort, the role of female pilots was re-examined. At first, women in the United States and Canada were considered too weak to handle the controls of military aircraft such as the huge B-17 bombers. French women, too, were told to forget flying and to concentrate on knitting warm clothes for soldiers.

In Germany, women were not allowed to fly in combat, but they did fly airplanes from factories to battlefields. Although they were not officially in the military, some women tested the fast and deadly fighter aircraft used by the *Luftwaffe*, the German air force. One of these pilots was Hanna Reitsch. Reitsch became the first pilot to cross the Alps in an engineless airplane or *glider*. During the war, she became the first woman to test fighters and helicopters as part of the German offensive.

By contrast, Soviet women actually flew combat missions and served in the military during World War II. In open-cockpit

form a women's section of the Air Transport Auxiliary (ATA). The ATA ferried aircraft from factories to air bases, and back from battle for repairs. From 1940 until the end of the war, the ferry pilots flew many kinds of aircraft from England to wherever they were needed. These pilots risked being shot down by enemy aircraft, flew through deadly thunderstorms, and flew damaged and unreliable airplanes. Out of 100 female pilots, 15 were killed flying for the ATA, including Amy Johnson.

In 1942, after the United States had entered World War II, word came from Henry "Hap" Arnold, the commanding general of the U.S. Army Air Corps, that American women with a commercial pilot's license and 500 hours of flying time would be accepted for service in England's ATA. The woman who persuaded Arnold to let the women serve was a gutsy, outspoken American pilot named Jacqueline Cochran.

biplanes, they dodged deadly antiaircraft fire to bomb German troops, railroads, and supply depots. Other Soviet women flew food to male soldiers trapped behind enemy lines. After the war, 23 of these women were honored with the title "Hero of the Soviet Union."

The person responsible for getting female pilots involved in the British war effort was Pauline Gower, daughter of a distinguished member of Great Britain's Parliament. A pilot herself, Gower had owned an air-taxi service in the 1930s. With her father's help, she persuaded the British government to let her

Jackie Cochran with a Lockheed C-140 Jetstar

JACQUELINE COCHRAN
Fastest Woman Alive

Jackie Cochran never knew who her parents were or exactly when she was born. "Cochran" was a name she took from a telephone book as a teenager. Her earliest memories go back to age four (probably about 1909), when she lived with a foster family in the sawmill towns of northern Florida. No one ever told Jackie how she came to live there. She remembers that her clothes were made from old flour sacks and she had no shoes. Many times she would search the woods for berries and pine nuts just to have something to eat.

When she was eight, Jackie moved with her foster family to Columbus, Georgia, where they hoped to find better paying jobs than those they had had in the sawmills.

Jackie took a job in a cotton mill, carrying large bobbins of yarn from the bins to the weavers. Most of her earnings went to help feed her family, but Jackie did manage to save enough for her first shoes, a secondhand pair of high heels purchased from a street peddler. Jackie dreamed of having a whole wardrobe of glamorous clothes. By age 10, she was promoted to inspection room supervisor at the cotton mill. She told everyone that someday she would be rich.

Two years later, Jackie left home and the mill and found a job as a housekeeper for a woman named Richler, who owned three beauty shops. In addition to keeping house, Jackie worked as an assistant at Mrs. Richler's shops. She learned to make hairpieces, give permanent waves, mix dyes, and color hair. She saved her money, and at age 15, she moved to Montgomery, Alabama, to find a better paying job in a larger salon.

Eventually Jackie decided that she had enough skill as a hairdresser to make a living in New York. She longed for excitement and thought that she could find it in New York City. Jackie landed a job at Antoine's, a prestigious salon inside Saks Fifth Avenue.

The Birth of an Aviator

In 1932 Jackie Cochran decided to quit Antoine's and take a job as a sales representative for a cosmetics company. Rather than waste precious time driving, Jackie wanted to cover her sales territory by flying from customer to customer. So she took flying lessons. But she didn't count on the fact that she would love flying for its own sake. As she wrote in her autobiography, *The Stars at Noon*, ". . . when I paid for my first [flying] lesson, a beauty operator ceased to exist and an aviator was born."

Two days after her first lesson, Jackie made her first solo flight over Long Island. Within three weeks, she had a private pilot's license. Jackie took the test orally because she couldn't read or write very well. Having to help support her foster family had limited her to only one year of formal schooling.

Jackie always wanted to be the best at everything she tried. She was determined to earn her *instrument rating*. This aviation rating is given to pilots who can fly using only the airplane's instruments for guidance—without looking out the window to see if the airplane is level with the horizon, where it is headed, or how high it is flying. These skills are important for a pilot flying through clouds or flying at night. With her earnings as a beautician, Jackie paid for more advanced flying lessons and received her instrument rating. Now she could fly even when visibility was poor.

In 1933 Jackie started a company in New York called Jacqueline Cochran Cosmetics. Cochran was particular about her appearance. Often she was seen applying lipstick and combing her hair before getting out of the cockpit. One of her company's first products was a skin moisturizer called Flowing Velvet. Jackie invented it because of her own problems keeping her skin moist when she was flying. She also designed hair dyes that customers could mix themselves and cream bases for makeup.

In 1936 Jackie married businessman Floyd Odlum. The couple moved to a 12-room apartment in Manhattan that was decorated with paintings of the airplanes Jackie had flown. Jackie and Floyd also bought a ranch in the southern California desert.

Named for aircraft company owner Vincent Bendix, the Bendix Cross-Country Air Race has been called the Kentucky Derby of aviation. In 1938 Jackie won the Bendix. Flying a Seversky Pursuit, she traveled from Burbank, California, to Cleveland, Ohio, in 8 hours, 10 minutes, and 31 seconds—at an average speed of 250 miles per hour (402 km/h). After receiving the winner's trophy from Vincent Bendix, Jackie climbed back into the cockpit and continued on to Bendix Airport in New Jersey, setting a women's west-to-east transcontinental record of 10 hours, 7 minutes, and 10 seconds.

The next year, Jackie set a women's U.S.

Vincent Bendix congratulates Jackie after the 1938 Bendix Air Race.

altitude record of 30,052 feet (9,015 m) over Palm Springs, California. She also set an international women's speed record that year of 306 miles per hour (489 km/h). In 1940 she set a new record in her Seversky Pursuit of 332 miles per hour (531 km/h). This was faster than any man or woman had ever flown.

Wartime Pilot

By 1941 Great Britain was under attack by Germany and needed bombers from the United States. Clayton Knight of the British Ferry Command suggested to Cochran that she help fly the bombers to England. Jackie leapt at the chance to gain experience in heavy aircraft and become the first woman to fly a bomber to Great Britain.

After 25 hours of instruction in a Lockheed Lodestar, Jackie felt ready to be tested, or "checked out," in the aircraft. But a British Bomber Service boss said that male ferry pilot crews would never agree to fly with a woman. Cochran couldn't handle a heavy bomber, he said, and would probably violate the code of secrecy required of pilots on such flights. Jackie was persistent, however, and finally, after a letter-perfect checkout, it was agreed that she could fly the bomber. Even so, a male copilot would be present to handle the aircraft during takeoff and landing, when the "heavy" work of using a hand brake was necessary. Cochran was furious at this insult, but she agreed to make the flight anyway.

When Jackie returned to the United States, President Franklin D. Roosevelt invited her to lunch. He wanted to know how female pilots could better help with the war effort. Cochran outlined her plan for a program that would recruit and train women to fly military aircraft. Henry Arnold, commanding general of the U.S. Army Air Corps (there was no separate United States Air Force then), was very much against the idea of allowing women into the military. He said that there would be too many problems training and housing the women.

As usual, Jackie refused to give up. She pointed out that by having women fly airplanes where they were needed, more men would be freed up for combat duty. Arnold finally agreed to let 25 American women join the Air Transport Auxiliary (ATA) in England. Jackie was in charge of selecting them.

All but one of the 25 female pilots returned home alive after their 18-month duty. The women flew as many as five different aircraft in a single day, landing and taking off in very difficult conditions such as muddy fields and bad weather. Often the women read the manual on how to fly the airplane while waiting to be cleared for takeoff.

The British program was so successful in freeing men for combat that General Arnold organized a group in the United States called the Women Airforce Service Pilots (WASPs). He asked Cochran to become director of flight training for the group. The WASPs would serve as ferry, or transport, pilots

Female pilots were eager to contribute to the war effort. Over 25,000 women applied to fly for the WASPs. Only 1,078 women made it into the program.

within the United States. They would also tow targets behind their airplanes for student antiaircraft gunners to shoot at (a dangerous job if the gunner missed the target and hit the aircraft). They would test new aircraft and fly during the day and night so that radar and searchlight operators could practice tracking them. But their favorite activity was simulated *strafing*—diving at supply trucks, chow lines, and other ground targets and pretending to shoot them with machine-gun fire while antiaircraft gunners tracked them.

Almost as soon as the new program was announced, Cochran had more than 25,000 applications from female pilots. Over one thousand women made it through the difficult training program.

Rather than wait for Congress to pass a bill making the WASPs an official part of the military, Cochran agreed that the women would be employed as civilians. This would allow them to start flying sooner, before the war ended. Unfortunately, two years later, Congress finally voted *not* to make the WASPs part of the military.

Although the WASPs flew as regularly and for as many hours as did male military pilots, they were denied veterans' benefits. The

Jackie Cochran (left) and General Hap Arnold congratulate the WASPs as they receive their pilots' wings.

WASP program was disbanded on December 20, 1944. Unemployed male pilots across the country protested that women had taken "their" jobs.

It was not until 1977 that Congress passed a bill saying that the WASPs had served in active military duty during World War II and thus were eligible for veterans' benefits. The Navy opened its flight training program to women in 1973, and the Air Force followed in 1976, but women in the military still do not fly in combat missions.

A Courageous Test Pilot

After the war was over, Cochran returned to her cosmetics business. She flew about 90,000 miles (144,000 km) per year, visiting stores that sold her products. She also resumed her racing career in 1946. Flying a P-51 Mustang, a sturdy fighter plane used extensively in the war, she came in second in that year's Bendix race—flying an average speed of 420 miles per hour (672 km/h).

Between 1946 and 1950, Cochran set several speed records. These flights tested the limits of many new high-speed aircraft. One fighter, the P-43, would shake and bump up and down at high speeds—then the motor and controls would quit working. As soon as Cochran lowered the *flaps* (hinged sections on the wings that help slow the airplane), the engine restarted, and the aircraft stopped shaking. An aerodynamics expert explained to her that when an aircraft was pushed faster than it was made to go, the surge in air pressure would start to crush the airplane. Cochran's test flights helped engineers learn that to fly faster than the speed of sound, stronger airplanes would be needed.

To honor her work with the WASPs, her speed and altitude records, and her work as a test pilot, Jackie Cochran was presented with the prestigious Clifford B. Harmon Trophy and named the outstanding female pilot of the 1940s.

Jackie Cochran receives the Harmon Trophy.

Jacqueline Auriol climbs out of the Mirage III jet, a Mach 2 airplane.

Two Jacquelines: A Friendly Rivalry

Jackie Cochran had a friendly but determined rival in the French pilot Jacqueline Auriol. In the tradition of many female flyers of the 1940s, Auriol's first step toward a career in aviation was to break a record. Auriol was the daughter-in-law of the president of France. A good friend who happened to be the chief of staff of the French air force loaned her a Vampire fighter jet to break Jackie Cochran's women's world speed record of 441 miles per hour (706 km/h).

Auriol took 14 training flights in the high-speed jet. On May 11, 1951, she flew 510 miles per hour (816 km/h) over a 62-mile (100-km) circular course, setting a new women's record. Jackie Cochran responded by nominating Auriol for the Harmon Trophy for the outstanding female pilot of the year, which she won.

After such a stunning performance, Auriol was accepted for training as a test pilot in Brétigny, France. In 16 months, she became a full-fledged civilian test pilot. She was 35 years old.

Mach 1

The 1950s marked the beginning of the jet age, and Jackie Cochran was determined not to be left flying propeller-driven airplanes. The new, faster *jet aircraft* were thrust forward when gases under pressure were expelled out the rear of the engines. Cochran wanted to go into history as the first woman to break the *sound barrier*—or fly faster than the speed of sound. The speed of sound is called "Mach 1." Sound travels more slowly—as low as 650 miles per hour (1,040 km/h)—in cold air. In warm air, it can travel close to 800 miles per hour (1,280 km/h). She would need a fast airplane to break the record. But Cochran was a civilian and therefore could not fly Air Force jets (after World War II, the Air Force became a separate branch of the U.S. military). So Cochran got a private firm, Canadair (owned by her husband), to hire her to test their F-86 Sabrejet—one of the fastest airplanes there was in 1953.

For her training in the F-86 Sabrejet, Jackie wanted the best test pilot available. She chose Chuck Yeager, a major in the U.S. Air Force who had himself broken the sound barrier in a very different kind of airplane, the X-1, in 1947.

When the sound barrier is broken, people on the ground hear a loud *sonic boom*. When an aircraft travels at a supersonic speed, it pushes a wave of air in front of it. The pressure in the wave becomes so great at this speed that when the wave of air reaches the ground, it creates a loud boom.

Cochran and Yeager began by practicing in T-33 jet trainers until Jackie knew exactly how to fly the jet and navigate the course. Then Yeager had Jackie practice in the F-86 until she could fly it perfectly. Yeager flew "chase"— that is, he went up with her in another F-86 each time she flew and evaluated her flying technique. Finally Jackie was ready

to see if she could handle the aircraft at Mach 1.

The noise from the sleek, silver jet was deafening as Jackie Cochran throttled up the engines of Canadair's F-86 Sabrejet and headed skyward. She climbed to 45,000 feet (13,500 m) and then began her power dive. She pushed the throttle to full power and headed almost straight down toward the earth.

She radioed to Yeager, who was watching from another jet, "OK, it's [Mach] .97, .98, .99." The ground crew heard a loud boom announcing her success. But Jackie couldn't even hear the jet's engine. She was flying faster than the sound waves could reach her— more than 650 miles per hour (1,040 km/h). Happy but tired, she pulled out of the dive and into level flight at 18,000 feet (5,400 m). She felt a powerful shaking sensation as the aircraft slowed down, going back through the barrier. A few minutes later, Jackie landed back at Edwards Air Force Base in the Mojave Desert of southern California. Almost instantly she was surrounded by fellow pilots and bystanders, each wanting to be the first to congratulate the fastest woman alive.

For the official FAI record, Jackie had to fly a 62-mile (100-km) circular course at 35,000 feet (10,500 m). The course was like a racetrack in the sky, a quarter of a mile wide. If she deviated from the course in any way, her record would be disqualified. She had to fly this specific course so that FAI recording devices could clock an official

Chuck Yeager, the first man to fly faster than the speed of sound, helped Jackie prepare for her record-breaking flight in the F-86 Sabrejet.

speed. Jackie broke all previous speed records for men and women by going 653 miles per hour (1,044 km/h) around the course. That year, Cochran was presented with another Harmon Trophy as the outstanding female pilot of 1953.

Jacqueline Auriol also loved fast airplanes. A few months after Jackie Cochran broke the sound barrier, Auriol followed suit. Not long after that, she flew twice the speed of sound, or Mach 2, in the incredibly fast Mirage III, which could fly 1,500 miles per hour (2,400 km/h) and climb to 40,000 feet (12,000 m) in three minutes. From 1951 until Auriol stopped trying for records in 1963, she and Cochran passed the title of "fastest woman alive" back and forth.

Even though she was now more than 50 years old, Jackie Cochran never slowed down. After several years test-flying T-38 jet trainers for the aircraft manufacturer Northrop, she signed on with Lockheed to fly a Mach 2 airplane, the F-104 Starfighter. Her job was not just to set records, but to find out how fast the F-104 could go and still perform well. On May 4, 1964, on a 9-mile (15-km) straightaway course, Jackie set a women's international speed record of 1,429 miles per hour (2,286 km/h)!

Jackie Cochran's flying career came to an abrupt end in 1970, when she started having fainting spells. Friends rushed her to the Lovelace Clinic in Albuquerque, New Mexico, where a pacemaker was implanted in Jackie's chest to help her heart keep its normal beat. Her heart rate had been dipping very low, causing her to black out. She was not able to fly any longer. Returning to the Odlum-Cochran ranch in southern California, she couldn't look into the desert sky that had been her second home without crying. Besides her happy 40-year marriage to Floyd Odlum, flying had been her life. In 1976 Floyd died, completely crippled by arthritis.

Jacqueline Cochran died on August 9, 1980. Her funeral was the simple one she had requested. Fourteen of her closest friends, including fellow pilot Chuck Yeager, were there. Yeager said, "Sometimes even Jackie Cochran couldn't believe what she had accomplished."

The female pilots who came after her were no less determined to break new ground for themselves and their fellow pilots. One of them dreamed of becoming an astronaut. Her name was Jerrie Cobb.

Jackie Cochran loved to fly fast airplanes like Northrop's T-38.

JERRIE COBB
Space Explorer

The old maroon and yellow Waco biplane droned through the air at 1,000 feet (300 m), its small wooden propeller turning steadily. Geraldyn (Jerrie) Cobb loved the feel of wind rushing through her long blonde hair as she sat in the rear seat of the cockpit. Although this was her first flying lesson, she felt certain that the sky would be her home for the rest of her life.

Her father, commercial pilot William Harvey Cobb, was her flight instructor. He signaled his daughter to push the control stick forward, and the aircraft descended. Then she pulled gently back on the stick until the nose pointed slightly upward, and the airplane ascended over the wheat fields outside Norman, Oklahoma. With the control stick to the right, Jerrie *banked*, or tipped, the airplane's wings for a right-hand turn. Sitting in the open cockpit behind her father, Jerrie practiced climbing, banking, and descending for over an hour. It was 1943, and she had just turned 12.

By the time she was 16 and legally eligible, Cobb had soloed and wanted to get a private pilot's license. To pay for lessons, she earned money any way she could—picking berries, working at a movie theater, waxing airplanes at a local airport, delivering drugstore prescriptions, and typing for a publisher. All her efforts were rewarded when, on March 5, 1948 (her 17th birthday), she obtained her private pilot's license.

Upon graduation from high school, Jerrie

announced her intention, not to go to college, but to fly professionally.

Jerrie's parents were disappointed, and her older sister thought she had lost her mind. With so many military pilots back from World War II, it was unlikely that a woman, especially one with only 200 hours in the air, would be able to find work as a pilot.

But Jerrie was confident. She supported herself by playing softball with a semi-professional women's team called the Sooner Queens. After three years with the Sooner Queens, Cobb had earned enough money to purchase her own airplane, a war surplus

Jerrie Cobb was eager to fly as far and as fast as she could. She dreamed that one day she would fly in space.

Fairchild PT-23. Jerrie had earned her commercial pilot's license on her 18th birthday, so she could now fly for pay.

With her new airplane and license, Jerrie got a job patrolling oil pipelines in Oklahoma, Kansas, and Missouri. Flying "low and slow" along the pipelines, she checked for escaping fumes and oil leaks.

Aviators must pass written tests and flight tests to become private pilots, instrument-rated pilots, commercial pilots, certified flight instructors, and airline transport pilots. After she received her commercial pilot's license, Jerrie looked forward to becoming a flight instructor. She built up flying time with her day job and then flew to Wichita, Kansas, at night to attend ground school. Here she received the classroom instruction needed for her flight instructor's certificate. She learned teaching techniques and took courses in aerodynamics, weather, and navigation. After passing a two-part written exam, and after more than two hours of demonstrating that she could pull a Cessna 140 out of the most dangerous situations, Jerrie Cobb received her flight instructor's certificate on her 21st birthday. Now she could teach others to fly.

She headed for Duncan, Oklahoma, and took a job as a flight and ground school instructor. Several male students commented that there was nothing a "dame" of 21 could teach them. However, when Jerrie Cobb stood in front of the class quoting whole passages from aviation manuals and lecturing on aerodynamics, weather, and navigation, they realized that it would serve them well to listen to her.

A Worldwide Ferry Pilot

In 1953 Cobb's life changed dramatically. Jerrie persuaded Jack Ford, the manager of an aircraft ferry service called Fleetway, to hire her to fly T-6s to South America—a job no male pilot would take. There, the aircraft would be used by the Peruvian air force. The third leg of the four-day trip would take Jerrie from Kingston, Jamaica, to Barranquilla, Colombia. The flight would have worried even the most seasoned pilot. The distance was 520 miles (832 km) with headwinds, and she would only have a 4-hour and 15-minute supply of gas to make a 4-hour trip. Therefore, she had to land the single-engined aircraft exactly at its destination—there would be no extra fuel to fly over the jungles or the shark-infested ocean to look for the airport. The last leg of the journey would take her over the high, rugged Andes Mountains. Often the peaks were obscured by clouds.

But Jerrie's biggest challenge on her first trip was not the landscape, it was the Ecuadorian government. Ecuador and Peru were not on friendly terms. So when Cobb made a refueling stop in Guayaquil, Ecuador, in a Peruvian air force airplane carrying bomb racks and machine guns, she was assumed to be an enemy spy and was thrown in jail. After 12 days, the U.S. government was finally able to gain her release. She received a hero's welcome when she finally landed at Peru's air force base near Lima.

Equipped with only a parachute, a life raft, emergency rations, a machete (a large knife), and a pistol, Cobb spent 1953 and

Jerrie Cobb at the controls over Oklahoma City.

1954 delivering T-6s to the Peruvian air force. Each round-trip took about 10 days. The blue and yellow T-6s with the female pilot became a familiar sight to Peruvians.

Then word came from Fleetway that the French government wanted some of the huge four-engine B-17 bombers that had been used by the United States during World War II. Fleetway chose Jerrie to ferry the bombers to France. Fleetway also asked her to fly large, bulky transport airplanes called C-46s to Calcutta, India. She flew almost constantly from then on, in one direction or the other.

By now Cobb was engaged to Jack Ford, the Fleetway flyer who had hired the "girl pilot," as he had called her at first. Much of their courtship was spent at airports all over the world, wherever their paths happened to cross. However, both Jerrie and Jack felt too committed to their jobs to take time to settle down together. Eventually, they broke their engagement. In 1959 Jack was killed when his airplane exploded over Wake Island in the Pacific.

From Ferry Pilot to Test Pilot

As a result of her breakup with Jack Ford in 1955, Jerrie resigned from Fleetway and went back to her family in Ponca City, Oklahoma. At her family's urging, she decided to put her life on a new track by setting distance and altitude records. Flying an Oklahoma-built Aero Commander, she traveled 1,504 miles (2,406 km) nonstop from Oklahoma City to Guatemala City,

At Tyndall Air Force Base in Panama City, Florida, Jerrie flew a TF 102 Delta Dagger faster than the speed of sound.

Guatemala, and back. She completed the flight in eight hours and five minutes and broke a record for that size airplane. On July 5, 1957, she set an altitude record of 30,560 feet (9,168 m) in another Aero Commander. Ironically, when Jerrie first asked for work as a pilot with Aero Design and Engineering (the company that made Aero Commanders), they refused because she was a woman. Finally on April 13, 1959, when she set a new speed record in an Aero Commander, the company hired her as a test pilot.

Later that year, at an Air Force Association conference in Miami, a meeting with Dr. W. Randolph Lovelace of the National Aeronautics and Space Administration (NASA) would change Jerrie's career. Lovelace was chairman of NASA's Life Sciences Committee for Project Mercury, NASA's first program to put people into space. The first group of astronauts was chosen in 1958. Seven men were selected as astronauts, but Dr. Lovelace was interested in the effects of space flight on women as well.

After talking with her about her experience as a pilot, Dr. Lovelace invited Cobb to become the first test subject for research on women as astronauts. The work would be hard, but Jerrie was overjoyed to be chosen. Her employers at Aero Design were less enthusiastic. Jerrie was now part of Aero Design's management team. If she went through the tests and was not chosen to fly in space, she would have lost valuable time

from her aviation career. But space flight had become Jerrie's dream, and she intended to pursue it, no matter what the cost.

Cobb Qualifies as an Astronaut

To train for the exhaustive tests at the Lovelace Foundation in Albuquerque, New Mexico, Jerrie ran 5 miles (8 km) per day and rode another 20 miles (32 km) on her exercise bike. She ate foods that were high in protein to build muscle.

For five days in February of 1960, Jerrie underwent tests to determine the health of her blood, lungs, heart, ears, nose, and throat. One of the hardest tests was the tilt table. She had to lie strapped to the table while it was tilted in all directions. An electrocardiogram and blood pressure cuff were strapped to her arm. Scientists wanted to be certain that Jerrie's heart and blood vessels were healthy, and that she would not faint if her body was positioned in an unusual way in space.

After the last test, one of the Lovelace Foundation doctors informed her that she had passed the Mercury astronaut tests. Dr. Lovelace told Jerrie that he felt that women would definitely be part of space flight in the future. He recommended that Jerrie fly to Lewis Research Center in Cleveland, Ohio, for another test—the Multi-Axis Spin Test.

This test was conducted in a padded chair, which could spin in three directions at the same time. The test was designed to

As an executive with Aero Design and Engineering, Jerrie Cobb was well known in the aviation industry. When NASA began to consider female pilots for space flight, Jerrie was the first woman chosen.

see if a pilot could control a space capsule under conditions of *pitch* (a forward or backward somersault), *roll* (a wing-over-wing flip), and *yaw* (a side-to-side turn). These rotations happened at an increasing speed, until the chair was turning 30 revolutions per minute in all three directions. For the pilot, it was like turning somersaults and spinning like a top at the same time. The pilot could stop the chair from rotating by using a hand control. Jerrie's ability to control the "capsule" was pronounced excellent.

Scientists also wanted to check her ability to remain isolated for long periods. Jerrie agreed to be put in the underground isolation water tank in Oklahoma City. Subjects were told to stay in the tank "as long as they could stand it." With only her head above water, Jerrie floated in pitch blackness for 9 hours and 40 minutes. The men's record was only six and a half hours.

When Dr. Lovelace announced to the public that a woman named Jerrie Cobb was ready to fly in space, there was an avalanche of telephone calls and visits by reporters and photographers. Everyone wanted to know all about the "lady astronaut." Jerrie made several television appearances and was featured in *Life* magazine.

The next year, Cobb assisted Randolph Lovelace and Jackie Cochran, who was also involved in the project, in selecting more women for astronaut testing. The women were pilots from the Ninety-Nines, the international female pilots' association. Cochran

and Lovelace decided that women selected for testing should have a commercial pilot's license and 1,500 hours flying time. Thirty-one women met these qualifications, and ultimately 12 passed the Mercury astronaut tests. (They were nicknamed the "flats" because Cobb regularly addressed their letters: Dear *F*ellow *L*ady *A*stronaut *T*rainee.)

In May 1961, Cobb was called in for more testing at the Naval Air Station in Pensacola, Florida. Many of the tests, like the tilt table and the electrocardiogram, were familiar ones. Then came the "airborne EEG" (electroencephalogram). With this test, scientists wanted to check changes in Jerrie's brain waves while she flew under high G-forces (forces higher than that of gravity).

Jerrie sat in the copilot's seat of a single-engine attack airplane called a Douglas Skyraider, with 18 needles stuck to her head. As the pilot took the aircraft through rolls, dives, and loops, the EEG machine recorded Jerrie's brain waves.

Soon after that, Jerrie flew to Tulsa, where she attended the first NASA conference on the peaceful uses of space. When NASA administrator James Webb introduced her to the group, he surprised her with the announcement that she was being named as a consultant to NASA. Part of her assignment, he said, was to write a report on women's participation in the space program.

Jerrie mailed her report, which recommended that qualified women be included in the astronaut corps. But there was silence

Jerrie takes a look at the Mercury Space Capsule. Despite an appeal to Congress, women weren't allowed into the Mercury astronaut program.

The Project Mercury astronauts, front row, left to right: Walter Schirra, Jr., Donald Slayton, John Glenn, Jr., and Scott Carpenter; back row: Alan B. Shepard, Jr., Gus Grissom, and Gordon Cooper.

from NASA. Finally, NASA announced that while women would certainly be involved in space flight in the *future*, it was not going to train female astronauts for Project Mercury. NASA refused to accept the women, it said, because they had no experience as jet test pilots.

Jerrie was devastated but refused to give up. The 12 female candidates, including Jane Hart, whose husband was a senator from Michigan, called members of Congress to gain support. On July 17, 1962, Cobb and the other candidates spoke to members of the Committee on Science and Astronautics of the House of Representatives.

Cobb pointed out that not only had the women proven themselves to be just as physically and mentally capable of being astronauts as men, but they also weighed less, used less oxygen, and ate less—a clear advantage in a small space capsule. Women were also less prone to have heart attacks. Cobb urged that the United States be the first nation to send a woman into space. After two days of testimony from Cobb, Hart, NASA officials, and astronaut John Glenn (who was against sending a woman into space), the committee members urged NASA to reconsider. Meanwhile, a second group of astronauts, nine white males, had been chosen for Project Gemini.

President John F. Kennedy had declared that training female astronauts would delay the national goal of putting a *man* on the moon by the end of the decade. It was not

Astronauts Shannon Lucid, Rhea Seddon, Kathryn Sullivan, Judith Resnik, Anna Fisher, and Sally Ride pose with a '60s-era space suit. In 1983 Sally Ride became the first American woman to travel into space.

until 1972 that Congress passed an amendment to the Civil Rights Act of 1964 stating that federal agencies could not discriminate on the basis of sex, race, religion, or national origin. NASA, a federal agency, hired the first female astronauts in 1978. They were Sally Ride, Judy Resnik, Kathy Sullivan, Shannon Lucid, Anna Fisher, and Rhea Seddon.

Jerrie was deeply saddened by NASA's failure to choose women for space in the early 1960s. Since NASA decided not to use her talents as a pilot, Cobb moved to Brazil in 1963 to work as a missionary pilot—flying doctors, missionaries, and medical supplies into isolated jungle villages and returning to the city with villagers who needed hospital care.

Sheila Scott arrives in London after her first round-the-world flight. Goodwill messages collected along the way adorn the wing of Sheila's Piper Comanche.

SHEILA SCOTT
Over the Pole

When Sheila Scott announced that she was going to learn to fly, her friends laughed. Sheila had just failed her driving test for the second time, and her friends assumed she was joking. Never would they have guessed that Sheila would become the first European woman to fly solo around the earth at the equator and the first woman to fly over the North Pole.

Born in Worcestershire, England, in the early 1920s, Sheila Scott was very daring even as a child. She loved roller coaster rides, diving from the high dive, and—the gift she received for her sixth birthday—a ride in a yellow biplane.

Sheila became a nurse after high school and was stationed in London during World War II. When the war ended in 1945, Sheila met a film producer and decided to try acting. She hoped it would provide an escape from the sadness of caring for people who had been wounded in the London bombings. A vivacious woman, Sheila worked in theater until 1959. Then she announced that she was going to learn to fly.

Although she had been a daredevil, Sheila was frozen with fear during her first three flying lessons. But she ignored her fears until they disappeared. By 1960 she had her private pilot's license. Right away, she purchased an old World War II airplane called a Tiger Moth and had the interior reupholstered and the engine overhauled. Friends teased her when she had the airplane painted blue with silver

Sheila Scott, unable to pass her driver's test, chose to travel by air.

wings and made the interior white. They warned her that the white seats would soon be covered with oil and grease. Undaunted, Sheila named the old airplane *Myth*, the Greek word for a female moth. She and *Myth* spent the summer of 1960 flying to North America, Africa, and all around Europe.

After 300 hours of flying time, with her commercial pilot's license in hand, Sheila sold *Myth*. She borrowed a Piper Comanche, and in 36 hours, she broke 15 European speed records for a light aircraft. Airplanes under 12,500 pounds (5,625 kilograms) are considered light aircraft.

Scott Flies around the World Twice

By now Sheila had decided that she would make a career of breaking records. In 1966 no European woman had flown solo around the world via the equator. So Sheila Scott decided to become the first. Jerrie Mock and Joan Merriam Smith, both Americans, had completed the trip in 1964. Jerrie, flying a Cessna 180, had made the trip in 29 days; Joan flew a Piper Apache and took only 23 days.

Sheila chose a Piper Comanche 260 (which she named *Myth Too*) and took along her stuffed rabbit "Buck Tooth" for good luck. To see more of the world, she chose a 32,000-mile, (51,200-km), eastward route, instead of flying the minimum 22,000 miles (35,200 km) required by the FAI. The flight took 33 days and included several stops to refuel.

Everyone seemed to have fun watching Sheila's progress. Airline pilots radioed their greetings, women in Singapore gave her orchids, and Fiji Islanders gave her shell necklaces. In Damascus, Syria, well-wishers filled her cockpit with fragrant jasmine because the newspapers had mentioned that Sheila loved sweet-smelling perfume. Over

Australia, female pilots in the desert outback radioed their support. As the women talked to her from radios in their homes, Scott could see their small airplanes parked on private landing strips nearby. A group of light aircraft pilots escorted her to New Zealand as a show of support. Mayors presented her with keys to their cities when she landed in North America for refueling. Back home at the London airport, an airline captain welcomed her and congratulated her as he touched down on a parallel runway.

In addition to setting distance and speed records, Scott also loved to race. In December 1969, she entered the England to Australia Air Race. Five minutes after takeoff, she realized that she had lost the ability to transmit or receive on both her radios. Several hours later, she discovered that her *autopilot*, the instrument that can be set to keep the airplane on the proper course and altitude, was not working. She would have to fly the race manually; there would be no time to rest. Scott wondered if her aircraft had been tampered with— possibly by someone who had bet a lot of money that someone else would win the race. Five hours outside of Darwin, Australia, it began to rain hard. Scott had to fly just 30 feet (9 m) above the ocean to get under the low clouds and see where she was going. To make matters worse, her compass was no longer working, and she feared she might get lost. Although it was sweltering in the cabin, Scott kept her life jacket on.

Suddenly her radio came to life, and she overheard an air traffic controller giving an airliner instructions to Darwin. Other voices came through, but Sheila could not understand much. Then she saw some small islands below and circled each of them, looking for a place to land. Meanwhile, she overheard more voices on the radio talking about *her* as if she were dead! Using the transmission button on her radio, she sent a message that she was lost—using the special long and short beeps of Morse code. Snatches of replies came back, but nothing that would help her find Darwin.

In what seemed like nothing short of a miracle, Scott suddenly saw a runway beneath her. Upon landing, she learned that she was on one of Indonesia's 13,000 islands. Scott had a Christmas dinner of rice, dried deer meat, tomatoes, and tea with the local doctor and his family. After several days, when fuel had been flown in and one of her radios was fixed, Scott headed for Darwin. From Darwin, Sheila headed for Alice Springs, in the center of the Australian desert, and then over to the coastal city of Adelaide in South Australia. She was nearly delirious with fever from pushing herself so hard. Finally, on January 5, 1970, she crossed the finish line at Sydney's Bankstown Airport, finishing fourth in her aircraft's class. She continued on to the United States, where she had her airplane restored to its original good condition and then flew home to England, completing a second round-the-world trip.

"I Must Fly" aptly describes Sheila's approach to her aviation career.

On Top of the World

Undaunted by her hardships in the England to Australia Air Race, Sheila Scott dreamed of being the first person to fly across the North Pole in a light aircraft. Charles Blair, an ex-fighter pilot, had crossed the North Pole in a P-51 Mustang in 1951—but the Mustang wasn't a light aircraft. Scott took out a bank loan to pay for a twin-engine Piper Aztec. Her beloved *Myth Too* was the security for the loan.

She named the new aircraft *Mythre*. It was outfitted with very large fuel tanks that would hold enough gas to take Scott over the pole.

Sheila decided to start at the equatorial city of Nairobi, Kenya. She would then fly to England, Norway, over the true North Pole, and on to Anchorage, Alaska. From there she would continue to San Francisco; Honolulu, Hawaii; Fiji; Darwin, Australia; Madras, India; Athens, Greece; and back to London. This would be her third flight around the world. By flying from Nairobi to the North Pole and across the equator again at Canton Island in the Pacific, Sheila would be the first person to make an equator-to-equator flight via a pole.

During February of 1971, about six months before her flight, Scott visited an astronaut friend at Cape Kennedy to watch the launch of Apollo 14. The astronaut, Phil Chapman, commented to Sheila that her flight over the North Pole could be useful to scientists. Almost before she could agree, an eavesdropping reporter for CBS mentioned the idea to NASA officials in Washington—they *were* interested.

NASA wanted to use Sheila's flight to track sulfur dioxide, a pollutant produced by burning oil and coal. NASA's Goddard Space Flight Center in Greenbelt, Maryland, installed a receiver/transmitter called a Balloon Interrogation Package (BIP) in *Mythre*. The BIP would collect data on the amount of sulfur dioxide in the atmosphere along Scott's route, so that scientists could learn how this gas travels. The BIP would also record the temperature of Scott's aircraft equipment and note her altitude and location.

The scientists were also interested in how long-distance flight affects a pilot's mental alertness. Via satellite, scientists at Goddard would trigger a green light on Sheila's control panel. When the light went on, it would be Sheila's job to press a "ready to test" button. A red code number would then appear on a black box between her knees. Her task would be to punch in the code on a set of buttons. Her quickness and accuracy in doing so would be used as a test of her alertness. She nicknamed this her "monkey test." The data would be transmitted back to NASA via the *Nimbus* space satellite, which was orbiting the earth.

Since Scott was British, a British agency had to be involved with the flight. Britain's Royal Air Force (RAF) agreed to study Scott's sleep patterns to learn how lack of sleep affects a pilot. Sheila would get from zero to eight hours of sleep on any given night during her 55-day flight. Sometimes, the continuous daylight in the northern latitudes would keep her awake. Other times, tough flying conditions would make it necessary for her to be constantly aware of her situation. There wouldn't be time for sleep. Sheila was asked to track all her sleeping and waking times throughout the flight and record how she was feeling.

Scott spent a day at the RAF's Institute of Aviation Medicine, testing her arctic clothing and survival gear. For one test, she sat in a chamber wearing five layers of clothing and a mountaineering suit, as RAF technicians brought the air temperature down to -4°F (-20°C) and turned on a wind machine.

For survival gear, the RAF outfitted Sheila with a 1-ounce (28-gram) sleeping bag, a one-woman dinghy, a life jacket, and an emergency transmitter. A sheepskin cover for the pilot's seat would keep Scott warm in the northern latitudes and cool in the tropics.

At last all was ready. Sheila Scott took off for the "top of the world" on June 11, 1971, from Nairobi, Kenya. One of the BIP's first readings over the Libyan Desert told Goddard scientists that there was a large amount of air pollution from burning gases in Middle Eastern oil fields.

On June 16, Scott landed in London for four days to have *Mythre* winterized. Returning to her apartment, she was dismayed to learn that it had been broken into. All her trophies and souvenirs from past races and record-setting flights had been stolen. The suitcases for her polar gear and the videotape camera with which she was supposed to film the polar regions were also gone. Scott had planned to sell the films to help pay for the trip, and she never recovered financially from this loss. Although disheartened, she decided to continue on. Her desire for knowledge and the record was stronger than her disappointment.

On June 22, 1971, with clear weather, a winterized aircraft, and a reorganized apartment, Scott prepared to take off for her next refueling stop: Bodo, Norway—inside the Arctic Circle. She would need so much gear for the very cold part of her flight that she had to climb into the cockpit and have the engineers pack her gear around her. Buck Tooth the rabbit sat on top of everything.

Mythre rolled faster and faster along the tarmac, a runway made of crushed stone and tar, until it reached a ground speed of 112 miles per hour (179 km/h). Sheila eased the throttle forward. The aircraft, with its heavy load of fuel, headed over the blackened chimneys of northern London.

An hour and a half later, the Piper Aztec crossed the southern tip of Norway. Its magnetic compass was swinging crazily because Sheila was flying so close to the magnetic North Pole. Since Sheila could not rely on her magnetic compass, she also carried a sun compass that was not affected by the pull of the pole.

A green light flashed in the cabin, reminding Scott that she was not alone. Scientists at Goddard were tracking her progress. Now they knew that she was crossing the Arctic Circle. Above this latitude line, it is dark for almost 24 hours a day in the winter and light for almost 24 hours a day during the summer. Since it was summer, Sheila would be flying in near-continuous daylight. Below her, Norwegians were celebrating Midsummer's Eve, the night before the first full day of sunlight in the Arctic Circle. At 10:30 P.M., she landed in Bodo. The sun was high in the sky.

The next morning, Scott taxied out of Bodo, bound for Andoya, Norway, her last stop before she would fly over the North Pole. After an hour's rest in Andoya, Sheila

*An artist's conception of **Nimbus**, the communications satellite that transmitted information from Sheila's polar flight back to NASA and RAF scientists.*

Sheila, suited for arctic weather, and her twin-engined Piper Aztec, **Mythre**

put on five layers of clothing. A harness that would measure her heart rate was taped to her skin.

Over the cold waters of the Arctic Ocean, Scott noticed that she was not flying as fast as she should be if she was going to make it to Alaska with the fuel she had on board. The trouble was a nosewheel (part of the landing gear) stuck in the down position. The door that enclosed this wheel at the front of the aircraft had come open. The wheel was acting as resistance against the wind and slowing her down. Sheila was able to activate the mechanism that retracted the wheel and closed the door. But soon the wheel came down again, and *Mythre* slowed.

The airplane was using too much fuel. To add to Sheila's problems, her autopilot broke. She had to fly the aircraft manually at all times—an exhausting situation. Sheila could not make it to Alaska on the fuel that was left, so she landed for refueling on a gravel runway in Nord, Greenland, at a Danish weather station. There were huge snowbanks on either side of her. Because she was flying through near-continuous daylight, Sheila had been awake for 40 hours without realizing it. When she was offered a bed, she slept soundly.

Late in the morning of June 28, rested and refueled, Scott took off. Burdened with its heavy fuel tanks, *Mythre* headed skyward, bound for the North Pole and then Barrow, Alaska.

At 9,000 feet (2,700 m), with an outside air temperature of 16° F (-9°C), Scott's aircraft, including the windshield, had become covered with ice. The nosewheel continued to fall into a downward position, and Sheila had to struggle with the frozen controls to bring it up. In spite of layers of clothing, she became very cold. To turn on the cabin heat would mean using precious fuel. Sheila radioed via the *Nimbus* satellite that she was "Pole minus 20 minutes and still counting."

By a method called "dead reckoning," based on time in the air and air speed, Sheila calculated that she was crossing the true North Pole. *Nimbus* later confirmed her calculation. "I'm on top of the world," Scott shouted into the mike.

"Say again," replied Nord. They wanted to make certain they had heard her correctly. She radioed back to the weather station, asking them to confirm her position. But there was no reply. Her radio had blacked out. Because of the high magnetic activity over the poles, arctic radio blackout is common.

Using her sun compass and dead reckoning, Sheila could only hope that she was on course. Seventeen hours after leaving Nord, Scott heard a voice on the radio from Barrow, Alaska, directing her to the runway. After flying over miles of tundra, she was overjoyed to see the huts in the village of Barrow, home of the Naval Arctic Research Laboratory.

As she stepped out onto the metal runway, dozens of people rushed to offer congratulations to the first person to pilot a light aircraft over the North Pole. Goddard scientists telephoned their congratulations.

The most difficult part of Scott's journey was over. Now she would be flying into warmer air. She would be in constant radio contact with the ground, and her magnetic compass would work properly. Her route would take her to San Francisco, Hawaii, Fiji, Darwin, and home to England—for a total of 34,000 miles (54,400 km). Sheila arrived in London on August 8, 1971, beating the Darwin-to-London time set in 1934 by the famed New Zealand pilot Jean Batten.

From Scott's flight, NASA learned that there was a large band of sulfur dioxide over the North Pole. With this information, they developed several new airborne pollution sensors, which they used to discover how far and fast pollution travels.

NASA also used Scott's flight to test their Global Rescue Alarm Net (GRAN). Although no longer in use, GRAN was used to locate, via three satellites, the radio signal of travelers in distress anywhere in the world.

After a rest at her London apartment, during which she found it impossible to resume a normal sleep pattern for several days, Scott flew in *Mythre* to Washington to meet with the NASA scientists who had monitored her flight. Unfortunately, while Scott was in Washington, Hurricane Agnes hit the East Coast of the United States, and *Mythre* was reduced to a shell. Scott could not afford the extensive repairs needed, so she lost *Mythre* forever.

That same year, Sheila finally passed her driver's test, only to become involved in a car accident that left her nearly blind. After two years of operations, she gradually regained most of her eyesight, but she knew that her next dream—to fly over the South Pole—could never come true. Scott now lives in London and works as a writer, broadcaster, and lecturer.

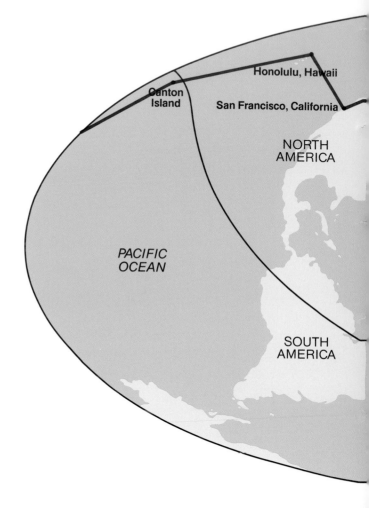

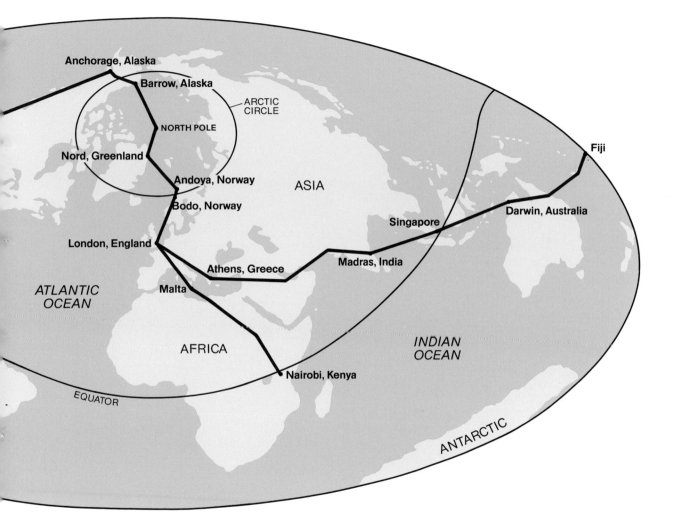

Sheila Scott's polar flight began in Nairobi, Kenya, and took her over the North Pole, around the world, and home to London.

BONNIE TIBURZI
Airline Pilot

"Well, that's quite an ambition, Bonnie. But it's not very practical. You know you can't really be an airline pilot. There aren't any women airline pilots."

The voice was that of Bonnie Tiburzi's high school guidance counselor; the year, 1967. Bonnie was to hear many voices of discouragement before she finally realized her dream of becoming the first female pilot to work for a major airline.

Bonnie's father, Gus, a former airline pilot himself, operated Tiburzi Airways near Danbury, Connecticut. Tiburzi Airways offered flight training, charter flights, and sightseeing trips. Twelve-year-old Bonnie and her 14-year-old brother Allan loved hanging around the airport and listening to military

pilots and other aviators tell stories of their daring air adventures. Bonnie understood the talk very well. Her father had been giving her flying lessons, and already she was familiar with the instrument panels of six different airplanes.

Unfortunately, Tiburzi Airways did not make enough money to support the family. Gus was forced to close the business, and the Tiburzis moved to Pompano Beach, Florida, to open a travel agency. However, even with her family out of the flying business, Bonnie's interest in aviation stayed with her.

With her parents' encouragement, Bonnie spent more than a year in France working as a nanny. Mr. and Mrs. Tiburzi wanted Bonnie to do some serious thinking about her career. Before long, she knew the answer. She wrote to her parents that she wanted to put all of her time and energy into becoming an airline pilot. In reply, her father sent her his old flight computer in its worn leather case and his aviator glasses. Bonnie was deeply pleased at her father's confidence in her.

In 1968 Bonnie returned to the United States, got a job in a dress shop, and began weekly flying lessons. Within three months, she had made her first solo flight as a student pilot. She would need at least another 40 hours of flying time to get her private pilot's license. To save the money for lessons, Bonnie moved in with her parents and worked at Tiburzi Travel. In eight months, she had her private pilot's license and could fly with friends and family under good weather conditions.

Bonnie's next step was to get a commercial pilot's license. She needed 200 hours of flight time for this rating. Slowly, she built up time by flying airplanes for Pompano Aviation from one Florida city to another, wherever they were needed. But Bonnie felt as if the hours were not accumulating fast enough and that she would never get her commercial pilot's license. In 1970 she headed back to Europe, looking for opportunities to fly.

She joined friends in Brussels and designed a job for herself. The local airport housed a small charter company, Publi-Air, which flew small groups of people on special business flights. Bonnie's job was to convince American companies to fly with Publi-Air. In return, Bonnie would fly the charters as a copilot—not for money, but for flight time. Upon reaching cruising altitude, she doubled as a cabin attendant for the businesspeople on board.

Through her new job, Bonnie met a flight instructor who had a flight simulator. The simulator is an earthbound model of an airplane's cockpit. Practicing in the simulator would prepare Bonnie to fly large, sophisticated, multiengine airplanes. But time in the simulator was expensive. The flight instructor's wife wanted to learn English, so Tiburzi agreed to give English lessons in exchange for training time in the simulator. By February 1971, Bonnie had passed her tests and logged enough hours to become a commercial pilot.

Back in Pompano Beach, Bonnie became a flight instructor. She also did a lot of charter flying, getting checked out, or tested, in larger and larger airplanes and building up flying time. The work hours were long. Many of the charter flights started early in the morning, and often Bonnie had to wait for her passengers at their destination and return with them late at night. Other days, she stayed late at the airport to teach student pilots after they got off work.

Once again, Bonnie heard a voice of discouragement. It came from her boyfriend. "Why not settle for becoming a corporate pilot," he suggested. Bonnie replied that she didn't want to open up the airport, write up

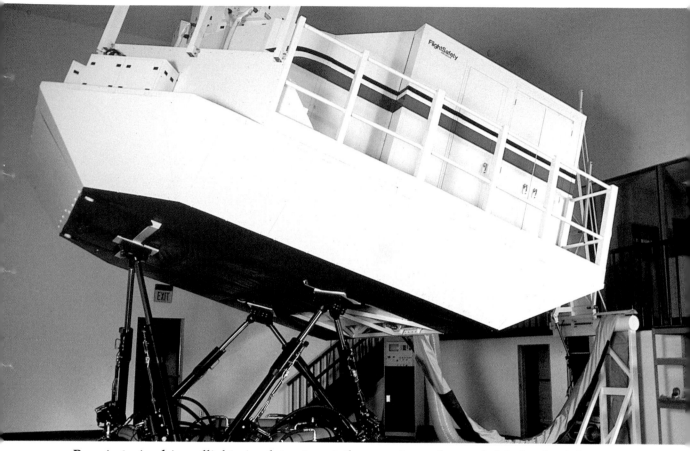

Bonnie trained in a flight simulator to get the experience she needed to land a job as an airline pilot. Once accepted by American Airlines, Bonnie's training was not over. She went back into the simulator for hours of practice.

tickets, or carry baggage—all things that a corporate pilot must do. She wanted only to fly—and for a high salary. Only working as a pilot for a major airline would give her what she wanted.

Bonnie wrote to all the major airlines and every local airline listed in the *Official Airline Guide*. Several airlines replied that they were not hiring at the moment, but many requested that she fill out an application for employment. Finally, in February 1973, Bonnie got a call from the American Airlines recruiting office in Dallas, Texas. They invited her to come in for an interview.

During her two-day visit, Bonnie discussed the different kinds of aircraft she had flown, underwent an eight-hour physical exam, and was tested on her math and English skills.

Then she returned home to await the results. American Airlines was hiring 214 pilots, and there were 15,000 applicants. Several were former Blue Angels, the Navy's top pilots. Many had college degrees. Bonnie had never liked school and had not gone to college. She was very pessimistic about her chances of being hired.

A Woman in the Cockpit

Bonnie was surprised and overjoyed, therefore, to receive a telegram asking her to report to the American Airlines training center for 8 to 10 weeks of flight training, beginning on March 30, 1973. At age 24, Bonnie was the youngest student in the group and the first woman ever to be hired by a major airline. (That year, Frontier, a smaller airline, had also hired a female pilot, a woman named Emily Howell.)

New pilots start out as flight engineers. It is their job to make sure that the airplane's mechanical systems work properly. Bonnie would need to learn every detail about the Boeing 727 — its electrical, air conditioning, and hydraulic systems. She would also have to know how to fly and land the aircraft in an emergency. The flight engineer sits at a desk in back of the pilot and copilot.

In Dallas, Bonnie looked for the former Blue Angels and some of the other experienced pilots she had met at the interviews. Most of them were nowhere to be seen. She wondered out loud to an instructor if she had been hired over these more experienced pilots as a token woman.

The instructor was quick to stress that simply having 5,000 hours of flight time in military aircraft or working five years at a local airline wasn't necessarily the right experience. He said that American was looking for pilots who could learn the airline's particular flying techniques, so that all American pilots, copilots, and flight engineers could work as a smoothly functioning team. American didn't like retraining pilots who had flown elsewhere.

Her instructors at American had one more concern. In a large jet, should one or more engines fail, the aircraft will yaw, or turn, toward the dead engine. It takes a lot of leg strength to push the rudder pedals hard enough to steer the aircraft away from the yaw to put the aircraft back on course. Instructors were worried that Bonnie, and anyone else less than 5 feet, 10 inches (175 centimeters) and 140 pounds (63 kg), might not be strong enough to work the controls manually. Bonnie's work in the flight simulator put her instructors' fears to rest. Athletic Bonnie proved that she could hold the rudders in position with her feet, use the hand crank to adjust the airplane's flaps, and keep the aircraft's nose high enough to stay in the air but low enough to keep the aircraft from stalling.

While acting as flight engineer in the simulator, however, Bonnie found out that she couldn't reach a circuit breaker in the cockpit. She solved the problem by using a pair of pliers to pop the circuit breaker into place. The student airline pilots spent many hours in the simulator learning to cope with problems like this one, as well as instrument failure, dense fog, engine fires, and other emergencies. The students were expected to work together to solve the problems. After several weeks of ground school, Bonnie

The first female airline pilot made headlines. Reporters, photographers, and American Airline executives crowd around Bonnie at a press conference in Dallas.

passed her oral exam and put in 25 hours in the simulator.

After a successful check ride in a real Boeing 727 (without passengers), Bonnie's work at the training center was over. Now it was time for her "on-the-line check ride." The Boeing 727 would be loaded with passengers and cargo. Bonnie would be the junior member of a cockpit crew consisting of a pilot (captain), copilot (first officer), and flight engineer (second officer). As a newly trained airline pilot, Bonnie would be the flight engineer, and one of her instructors would observe her performance. The flight was from Dallas, Texas, to Tucson, Arizona. Unfortunately, the captain did not

Tiburzi is now the captain of a Boeing 727.

Photograph by Chris Sorensen

want to fly with a woman. Although the captain ignored her, Bonnie proceeded with her duties and the trip went smoothly.

Pictures of Bonnie as the first female pilot for a major airline appeared in many national newspapers and magazines. It seemed that everyone knew about her. At that time, Chicago's O'Hare airport had separate lounges for male pilots and female flight attendants. On a trip to O'Hare, Bonnie was pleased to see that underneath a sign over the pilots' lounge, which read "male crew members only," someone had written "and Bonnie too!" Soon after, crew lounges were made available to male and female pilots and flight attendants together.

July 27, 1979, was a very important day for Bonnie Tiburzi. She had returned to Dallas for four weeks of advanced training and was now an American Airlines copilot. As first officer, she sat in the right-hand seat and flew the aircraft for half of each trip.

By the end of 1973, there were four female airline pilots in the United States. In 1982 Piedmont Aviation pilot Cheryl Peters became the first female airline captain (Tiburzi had put off that honor for a few years so that she could stay based in New York with her husband and children), and in 1984 Lynn Rippelmeyer became the first woman to captain a Boeing 747 jumbo jet. By 1990 about 900 women were flying for major air carriers.

American's first all-female flight crew. Back row: pilots Tracy Prior, Beverly Bass, and Terry Clairidge. Front row: flight attendants Sally Houston, Beverly Donawa, Nancy Hayth, and Alice Chedister.

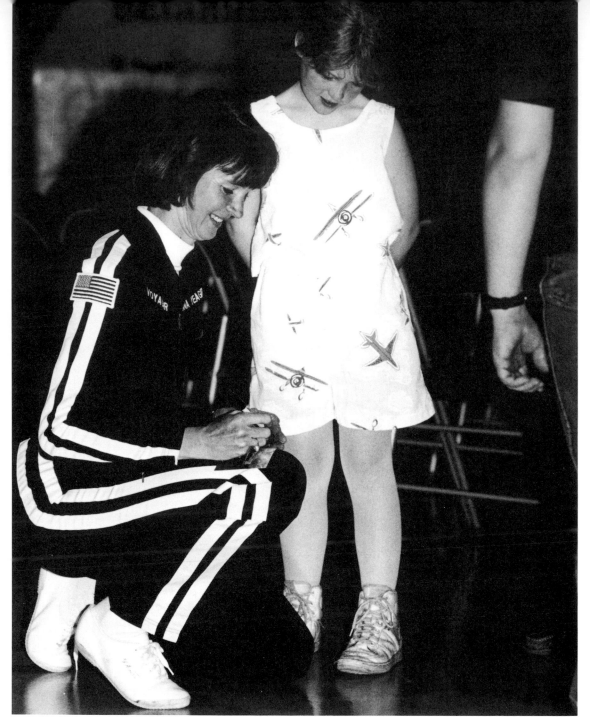

Jeana Yeager gives her autograph to a young aviation fan.

THE FUTURE

Many people went after aviation records during the 1920s and '30s, not only to secure a place in the record books, but also to test whether commercial aviation was possible. Pilots wanted to know whether an aircraft could fly nonstop from North America to Europe and fight strong headwinds to fly back across the Atlantic the other way. They also wanted to know how quickly airplanes could travel from one airport to another. Women like Beryl Markham and Amelia Earhart helped to answer these questions.

By the 1940s, the next challenge for female pilots was to gain equal status with men in the war effort. Although most women could not fly in combat, women did make a significant contribution during World War II by ferrying aircraft to wherever they were needed and helping to train combat pilots.

The big question of the 1950s was: how high and how fast can an aircraft be pushed before it ceases to function? Most of the test pilots were men who received free training in the military. But a few highly determined and skillful women like Jackie Cochran and Jacqueline Auriol were able to become civilian test pilots.

Some new records were set in the 1960s, 1970s, and 1980s. Sheila Scott contributed to our knowledge of pollution drift and pilot endurance with her flight over the North Pole. In December 1986, Jeana Yeager and her partner Dick Rutan set a record by flying around the world nonstop without refueling.

Jeana Yeager and her partner Dick Rutan traveled nonstop around the world in the ultra-light Voyager.

They flew in their long-winged, ultra-light *Voyager*. Their nine-day flight cost over $2 million, but they wanted to go for "the last big plum in aviation history," as Dick Rutan called it. It is likely that their flight will inspire airplane builders to create a new generation of ultra-light, fuel-efficient aircraft.

Women were accepted as pilots by the major airlines in the early 1970s, and as astronauts in the late 1970s. Many female astronauts have distinguished themselves in space flight, and it may not be long before a woman is named commander of a space shuttle.

NASA and the Air Force are working on a space plane that can fly into orbit without a boost from a rocket. It would fly through space at Mach 25 or about 16,250 miles per hour (26,000 km/h) and still be able to land on conventional runways. When the aircraft is tested in the year 2000, the first pilots will probably be combat-trained Air Force test pilots. The military has yet to allow female pilots to train for combat, but as soon as this training is available, a woman might be seen at the controls of the space plane.

Since the beginning of aviation history, women have shown courage in their desire to fly longer distances at faster speeds, pilot new kinds of aircraft, and explore new professions in the field of aviation. As aircraft become faster and more sophisticated, women will certainly be there flying them.

An artist's conception of the space airplane (above). A Navy aviator (left). Combat training is still not available to female aviators in the American military forces.

Louise Thaden receives the 1936 Bendix Trophy.

Index

A P-51 Mustang, one of the many military airplanes flown by the WASPs during World War II

Vampire fighter jet, 28

Amelia Earhart with* Flying Laboratory, *the airplane in which she attempted to fly around the world

ACKNOWLEDGMENTS

Photographs and illustrations are reproduced through the courtesy of: Royal Air Force, p. 1; Women Airforce Service Pilots, pp. 2, 25; Resource Center of the Ninety-Nines, pp. 6, 8, 9, 68; UPI/Bettman Newsphotos, pp. 10, 18, 48; Smithsonian Institution, pp. 12, 13, 14, 17 (top), 20, 23, 26, 27, 28, 31, 41, 46, 72; Schlesinger Library, p. 15; Experimental Aircraft Association, p. 17 (bottom); U.S. Air Force, pp. 30, 71; National Aeronautics and Space Administration, pp. 32, 34, 36, 37, 39, 42, 43, 51, 67 (top); Pictorial Parade, pp. 44, 52; Laura Westlund, pp. 54, 55; American Airlines, pp. 56, 61, 63; Patty McClain, FlightSafety International Inc., p. 59; Chris Sorensen, p. 62; Carl Schuppel, p. 64; Jim Koepnick, p. 66; U.S. Navy, p. 67 (bottom); Stouffer's Photo Service, p. 70.

Front cover photograph: U.S. Air Force.

Back cover photograph: Smithsonian Institution.